GOD AND GOLEM, Inc.

NORBERT WIENER

GOD AND GOLEM, Inc.

*A Comment on Certain Points where
Cybernetics Impinges on Religion*

1964

THE M.I.T. PRESS

*Massachusetts Institute of Technology
Cambridge, Massachusetts*

First M.I.T. Press Paperback Edition, March 1966
Second Paperback Edition, November 1969

Copyright © 1964 by
The Massachusetts Institute of Technology
All Rights Reserved

SBN 262 73011 1 (paperback)

Library of Congress Catalog Card Number: 64-16415
Printed in the United States of America

To Piet Hein
for encouragement and criticism

Preface

Some years ago, in *The Human Use of Human Beings*,* I gave an account of some of the ethical and sociological implications of my previous work *Cybernetics*,† the study of control and communication in machines and living beings. At that period, cybernetics was a relatively new idea, and neither the scientific nor the social implications had become fully clear. Now—some fifteen years later—cybernetics has made a certain social and scientific impact, and enough has happened to justify a new book in a related field.

The problem of unemployment arising from automatization is no longer conjectural, but has become a very vital difficulty of modern society. The cybernetic circle of ideas, from being a program for the future and a pious hope, is now a

* Wiener, N., *The Human Use of Human Beings; Cybernetics and Society*, Houghton Mifflin Company, Boston, 1950.

† Wiener, N., *Cybernetics, or Control and Communication in the Animal and the Machine*, The Technology Press and John Wiley & Sons, Inc., New York, 1948.

working technique in engineering, in biology, in medicine, and in sociology, and has undergone a great internal development.

I have given more than one series of lectures trying to outline the impingement of this circle of ideas on society, ethics, and religion, and I think the time has come to attempt a synthesis of my ideas in this direction, to consider more in detail the social consequences of cybernetics. This book is devoted to certain aspects of these consequences, in the discussion of which, although I retain the ideas and many of the comments which I made in the *Human Use of Human Beings,* I can consider the matter more in detail and more completely.

In this undertaking, I wish to acknowledge the great help I have received from the criticism of many friends on both sides of the Atlantic, especially from Mr. Piet Hein of Rungsted Kyst in Denmark, from Dr. Lawrence Frank of Belmont, Massachusetts, and from Professor Karl Deutsch of Yale University, as well as from many others. In addition, I wish to thank my secretary, Mrs. Eva-Maria Ritter, for her assistance in the preparation of this material.

I found an opportunity to elaborate my ideas in a course of lectures which I gave in January of

1962 at Yale University, and in a seminar that was held in the summer of 1962 at the Colloques Philosophiques Internationaux de Royaumont near Paris. However, this book, though containing material from my talks at both these places, has been completely rewritten and reorganized.

With gratitude to the many who have helped in this effort.

Norbert Wiener

Sandwich, New Hampshire
August 30, 1963

I

It is here my intention to discuss not religion and science as a whole but certain points in those sciences in which I have been interested—the communication and control sciences—which seem to me to be near that frontier on which science impinges upon religion. I wish to avoid those logical paradoxes that are bound to accompany the extreme (but usual) claims of religion to deal with absolutes. If we are to treat knowledge only in terms of Omniscience, power only in terms of Omnipotence, worship only in terms of the One Godhead, we shall find ourselves entangled in metaphysical subtleties before we shall have really embarked upon our study of the relations between religion and science.

Nevertheless, there are many questions concerning knowledge, power, and worship which do impinge upon some of the more recent developments of science, and which we may well discuss without entering upon these absolute notions, which are surrounded with so much emotion and reverence that it is quite impossible to enter upon them in a detached way. Knowledge is a fact, power is a fact, worship is a fact, and these facts are subject to human investigation quite apart from an accepted theology. As facts, these matters are subject to study, and in this study we may adduce our observations of knowledge, power, and worship in other fields, more accessible to the methods of the natural sciences, without at once demanding of the student a complete acceptance of the *"credo quia incredible est"* attitude.

It may be said that by starting in this way outside religion, I have already removed this discussion from being one of the relations between science and religion, which is suggested by the general trend of this essay. Therefore, I had better define my theme at the beginning, specify the corner of my subject in which I intend to remain, and disclaim those purposes that are alien to my specific task. As I have said, I have been working for several years on problems of communication and control, whether in machines or in living organisms; on the new engineering and physiological techniques attaching to these notions; and on the study of the consequences of these techniques for the achievement of human purposes. Knowledge is inextricably intertwined with communication, power with control, and the evaluation of human purposes with ethics and the whole normative side of religion. It is hence germane to a revised study of the relations between science and religion that we should re-examine our ideas of these matters in terms of the latest developments of theory and practical technique. This may not itself constitute a study of science and its relations to religion in the full sense, but it certainly constitutes an indispensable prolegomenon to such a study.

In a study of this sort, if it is to lead anywhere, we must disencumber ourselves of the superimposed layers of prejudice that we use nominally to protect the homage which we pay dignified and holy things but in fact, as often as not to relieve ourselves from the sense of unworthiness which we feel in looking unpleasant realities and dangerous comparisons in the face.

If this essay is to mean anything, it must be a real probing of real questions. The spirit in which it is to be undertaken is that of the operating room, not of the ceremonial feast of weeping about a corpse. Squeamishness is out of place here—it is even a blasphemy, like the bedside manners of the fashionable physician of the last century, with his black frock coat and the surgical needles hiding under the silk lapel of his coat.

Religion, whatever else it contains, has often something in itself of the closed front parlor of a New England farmhouse, with drawn blinds, wax flowers under a bell jar on the mantelpiece, gilded bulrushes surrounding grandfather's portrait on an easel, and a harmonium in black walnut, never played except at weddings or funerals. Or again, it is the moral counterpart of a Neapolitan hearse, one of those black plate-glass-windowed royal carriages, with their black-plumed stallions carrying even into death the assertion of status, or at any rate of the aspiration to status. Religion is a serious matter that we must separate sharply from any consideration of personal values of less significance than religion itself.

I have spoken of the layers of prejudice which encumber our approach to those problems in the vital common ground where science and religion come together: we must avoid discussing God and man in the same breath—that is blasphemy. Like Descartes, we must maintain the dignity of Man by treating him on a basis entirely different from that on which we treat the lower animals. Evolution and the origin of species are a desecration of human values; and as the earlier Darwinians found, to entertain these ideas is very dangerous for the scientist in a world fundamentally suspicious of science.

But even in the field of science, it is perilous to run counter to the accepted tables of precedence. On no account is it permissible to mention living beings and machines in the same breath. Living beings are living beings in all their parts; while machines are made of metals and other unorganized substances, with no fine structure relevant to their purposive or quasi-purposive function. Physics—or so it is generally supposed—takes no account of purpose; and the emergence of life is something totally new.

If we adhere to all these tabus, we may acquire a great reputation as conservative and sound thinkers, but we shall contribute very little to the further advance of knowledge. It is the part of the scientist—of the intelligent and honest man of letters and of the intelligent and honest clergyman as well—to entertain heretical and forbidden opinions experimentally, even if he is finally to reject them. Moreover, this rejection must not be taken for granted at the beginning and merely constitute an empty spiritual exercise, understood from the start to be no more than a game, in which one engages to show one's spiritual open-mindedness. It is a serious exercise, and should be undertaken in all earnestness: it is only when it involves a real risk of heresy that there is any point to it; and if heresy involves a risk of spiritual damnation, then this risk must be undertaken honestly and courageously. In the words of the Calvinist, "Are you willing to be damned for the greater glory of God?"

It is in this light of honest and searching criticism that we must regard an attitude which we have already mentioned, and which it is hard to avoid in discussions of religious matters—the evasion implied by the false superlative. I have already mentioned the intellectual difficulties arising out of the notions of omnipotence, omniscience, and the like. These appear in their crudest form in the question often asked by the scoffer who turns up uninvited at religious meetings: "Can God make a stone so heavy that He cannot lift it?" If He cannot, there is a limit to His power, or at least there appears to be; and if He can, this seems to constitute a limitation to His power too.

It is easy to dispose of this difficulty as a verbal quibble, but it is more. The paradox of this question is one of the many paradoxes that center about the notion of infinity, in its many forms. On the one hand, the least manipulation of the mathematically infinite introduces the notion of zero over zero, or infinity over infinity, or infinity times zero, or infinity minus infinity. These are called *indeterminate forms,* and the difficulty they conceal lies fundamentally in the fact that infinity does not conform to the ordinary conditions of a number or a quantity, so that ∞/∞ only means for the mathematician the limit of x/y, as x and y both tend to infinity. This may be 1 if $y = x$, 0 if $y = x^2$, or ∞ if $y = 1/x$, and so on.

Again, there is a different infinity which arises in counting. It can be shown that this notion too leads to paradoxes. How many numbers are in the class of all numbers? It can be shown that this is not a legitimate question, and that however one defines number, the number of all numbers is greater than any number. This is one of the Frege-Russell paradoxes and involves the complexities of the theory of types.

The fact is that the superlatives of Omnipotence and Omniscience are not true superlatives but merely loose ways of asserting very great power and very great knowledge. They express an emotion of reverence and not a metaphysically defensible statement. If God surpasseth the human intellect, and cannot be compassed by intellectual forms—and this is at least a defensible position—it is not intellectually honest to stultify the intellect itself by forcing God into intellectual forms which should have a very definite intellectual meaning. Thus, when we find limited situations that seem to cast light upon some of the statements generally made in religious books, it seems to me disingenuous to cast these aside because they do not have the absolute, infinite, and complete character which we are wont to attribute to religious utterances.

This statement gives the key to my purposes in the present book. I wish to take certain situations which have been discussed in religious books, and have a religious aspect, but possess a close analogy to other situations which belong to science, and in particular to the new science of cybernetics, the science of communication and control, whether in machines or in living organisms. I propose to use the limited analogies of cybernetic situations to cast a little light on the religious situations.

In doing this, I certainly shall have to force the religious situations somewhat into my cybernetic frame. I am quite conscious of the violence I must use in doing so. My excuse is that it is only through the knife of the anatomist that we have the science of anatomy, and that the knife of the anatomist is also an instrument which explores only by doing violence.

II

With these preliminary remarks, let me turn to the real theme of this little book.

There are at least three points in cybernetics which appear to me to be relevant to religious issues. One of these concerns machines which learn; one concerns machines which reproduce themselves; and one, the coordination of machine and man. I may say that such machines are known to exist. A program has been written by Dr. A. L. Samuel of the International Business Machines Corporation which allows a computer to play a game of checkers, and this computer learns, or at least appears to learn, to improve its game by its own experience.* There are certain statements

---

* Samuel, A. L., "Some Studies in Machine Learning, Using the Game of Checkers," *IBM Journal of Research and Development*, Vol. 3, 210–229 (July, 1959).

here which need confirmation, or at least clarification; and I shall devote one section of this book to this clarification.

Learning is a property that we often attribute exclusively to self-conscious systems, and almost always to living systems. It is a phenomenon that occurs in its most characteristic form in Man, and constitutes one of those attributes of Man which is most easily put in conjunction with those aspects of Man which are easily associated with his religious life. Indeed, it is hard to see how any non-learning being can be concerned with religion.

There is, however, another aspect of life which is naturally associated with religion. God is supposed to have made man in His own image, and the propagation of the race may also be interpreted as a function in which one living being makes another in its own image. In our desire to glorify God with respect to man and Man with respect to matter, it is thus natural to assume that machines cannot make other machines in their own image; that this is something associated with a sharp dichotomy of systems into living and non-living; and that it is moreover associated with the other dichotomy between creator and creature.

Is this, however, so? I shall devote a section of this book to certain considerations which, in my opinion, show that machines are very well able to make other machines in their own image. The subject upon which I am entering here is at once very technical and very precise. It should not be taken too seriously as an actual model of the process of biological generation, and even less as a complete model of divine creation; but neither is it negligible as to the light it throws upon both concepts.

These two parts of this book of lectures may be regarded as complementary the one to the other. The learning of the individual is a process that occurs in the life of the individual, in *ontogeny*. Biological reproduction is a phenomenon that occurs in the life of the race, in *phylogeny*, but the race learns even as the individual does. Darwinian natural selection is a kind of racial learning, which operates within the conditions imposed by the reproduction of the individual.

The third group of topics of this book is also related to problems of learning. It is concerned with the relations of the machine to the living being, and with systems involving elements of both kinds. As such, it involves considerations of a normative and, more specifically, of an ethical nature. It concerns some of the most important moral traps into which the present generation of human beings is likely to fall. It is also closely connected with a great body of human tradition and human legend, concerning magic and the like.

To begin with learning machines: an organized system may be said to be one which transforms a certain incoming message into an outgoing message, according to some principle of transformation. If this principle of transformation is subject to a certain criterion of merit of performance, and if the method of transformation is adjusted so as to tend to improve the performance of the system according to this criterion, the system is said to *learn*. A very simple type of system with an easily interpreted criterion of performance is a game, to be played according to fixed rules, where the criterion of performance is the successful winning of the game according to these rules.

Among such games are games with a perfect theory, which are not interesting. Nim, as defined by Bouton, and ticktacktoe are examples of such games. In these games, we not only can theoretically find a best policy for the playing of the game, but this policy is known in all its details. The player of such a game (either the first or the second) can always win, or at any rate draw, by following the policy indicated. In theory, any game can be brought to such a state—this is the idea of the late John von Neumann—but once a game has been brought to this state, it loses all interest, and need no longer be considered even as an amusement.

An omniscient being such as God would find chess and checkers (or draughts in England, or *dames* on the continent) to be examples of such von Neumann games, but as yet their complete theory has not been humanly worked out, and they still represent genuine contests of insight and intelligence. However, they are not played according to the manner suggested in the von Neumann theory. That is, we do not play them by making the best possible move, on the assumption that an opponent will make the best possible move, on the assumption that we shall make the best possible move, and so on, until one of the players wins or the game repeats itself. Indeed, to be able to play a game in the von Neumann manner is tantamount to possessing a complete theory of the game and to having reduced the game to a triviality.

The subject of learning, and in particular of machines that learn to play games, may seem somewhat remote from religion. Nevertheless, there is a religious problem to which those notions are relevant. This is the problem of the game between the Creator and a creature. This is the theme of the Book of Job, and of *Paradise Lost* as well.

In both these religious works the Devil is conceived as playing a game with God, for the soul of Job, or the souls of mankind in general. Now, according to orthodox Jewish and Christian views, the Devil is one of God's creatures. Any other supposition would lead to a moral dualism, savoring of Zoroastrianism and of that bastard offshoot of Zoroastrianism and Christianity which we call Manicheanism.

But if the Devil is one of God's creatures, the game that furnishes the content of the Book of Job and of *Paradise Lost* is a game between God and one of his creatures. Such a game seems at first sight a pitifully unequal contest. To play a game with an omnipotent, omniscient God is the act of a fool; and, as we are told, the Devil is a master of subtlety. Any uprising of the rebel angels is foredoomed to failure. It is not worth the Manfred-like rebellion of Satan to prove this point. Or else that omnipotence which needs to establish itself by celestial bombardments of thunderbolts is no omnipotence at all but merely a very great strength, and the Battle of the Angels might have ended with Satan on the celestial throne, and God cast down into eternal damnation.

Thus, if we do not lose ourselves in the dogmas of omnipotence and omniscience, the conflict between God and the Devil is a real conflict, and God is something less than absolutely omnipotent. He is actually engaged in a conflict with his creature, in which he may very well lose the game. And yet his creature is made by him according to his own free will, and would seem to derive all its possibility of action from God himself. Can God play a significant game with his own creature? Can *any* creator, even a limited one, play a significant game with his own creature?

In constructing machines with which he plays games, the inventor has arrogated to himself the function of a limited creator, whatever the nature of the game-playing device that he has constructed. This is in particular true in the case of game-playing machines that learn by experience. As I have already mentioned, such machines exist. How do these machines function? What degree of success have they had?

Instead of functioning after the pattern of the von Neumann game theory, they act in a manner much more closely analogous to the proceeding of the ordinary human game player. At each stage, they are subject to constraints that restrict the choice of the next move to one which is legal according to the rules of the game. One of these moves must be selected according to some normative criterion of good play.

Here, the experience of the human player of the game furnishes a number of clues to be used in picking out this criterion. In checkers or chess it is generally disadvantageous to lose pieces and generally advantageous to take an opponent's piece. The player who retains his mobility and right of choice, as well as the player who secures the command of a large number of squares, is usually better off than his opponent who has been careless in these respects.

These criteria of good play hold throughout the game, but there are other criteria that belong to a particular stage of the game. At the end of the game, when the pieces are sparse on the board, it becomes more difficult to close with the opponent for the kill. At the beginning of the game —and this is a far more important factor in chess than in checkers—the pieces are arranged in a way that tends to make them immobile and impotent, and a development is needed that will get them out of one another's way, both for offensive and defensive purposes. Furthermore, with the great variety of pieces in chess as compared with the poverty of checkers in this regard, there are in chess a large number of special criteria of good play, the importance of which has been proved by centuries of experience.

These considerations may be combined (either additively or in some more complicated way) to give a figure of merit for the next move to be played by the machine. This may be done in a somewhat arbitrary manner. Then the machine compares the figures of merit of the moves legally possible and chooses that move with the largest figure of merit. This gives one way of automatizing the next move.

This automatization of the next move is not necessarily, or even usually, an optimum choice, but it is a choice, and the machine can go on playing. To judge the merit of this way of mechanizing a game, one should divest oneself of all the images of mechanization belonging to the technical devices used, or the physical image of humanity as displayed by the ordinary game player. Luckily this is easy, for it is what we always do in correspondence chess.

In correspondence chess, one player sends the moves by mail to the other, so that the only connection between the two players is a written document. Even in this sort of chess, a skilled player soon develops an image of the personality of his opponent—of his *chess* personality, that is. He will learn if his opponent is hasty or careful; if he is easily tricked or subtle; if he learns the tricks of the other player, or can be fooled again and again by the same elementary strategy. All this is done, I repeat, with no further communication than the playing of the game itself.

From this point of view, the player, be he a man or a machine, who plays by a simple table of merit, chosen once for all and unalterable, will give the impression of a rigid chess personality. Once you have found out his weak point, you have found it out for all time. If a strategem has worked once against him, it will always work. A very small number of plays are enough to establish his technique.

So much for the mechanized player who does not learn. However, there is nothing to prevent a mechanized player from playing in a more intelligent way. For this he must keep a record of past games and past plays. Then, at the end of each game or each sequence of games of a determined sort, his mechanism is put to a totally different sort of use.

In building up the figure of merit, certain constants are introduced which might have been chosen differently. The relative importance of the command constant, the mobility constant, and the number-of-pieces constant might have been 10:3:2, instead of 9:4:4. The new use of the regulating machine is to examine games already played and, in view of the outcome of these, to give a figure of merit; not to the plays already made, but to the weighting chosen for the evaluation of these plays.

In this way, the figure of merit is continually being re-evaluated, in such a manner as to give a higher figure of merit for configurations occurring chiefly in winning games, and a lower figure of merit for situations occurring chiefly in losing games. The play will continue with this new figure of merit, which may be established in many ways differing in detail. The result will be that the game-playing machine will continually transform itself into a different machine, in accordance with the history of the actual play. In this, the experience and success, both of the machine and of its human opponent, will play a role.

In playing against such a machine, which absorbs part of its playing personality from its opponent, this playing personality will not be absolutely rigid. The opponent may find that stratagems which have worked in the past, will fail to work in the future. The machine may develop an uncanny canniness.

It may be said that all this unexpected intelligence of the machine has been built into it by its designer and programmer. This is true in one sense, but it need not be true that all of the new habits of the machine have been explicitly foreseen by him. If this were the case, he should have no difficulty in defeating his own creation. This is not in accordance with the actual history of Samuel's machine.

As a matter of fact, for a considerable period Samuel's machine was able to defeat him rather consistently, after a day or so of working in. It must be said that Samuel, by his own statement, was no checker expert to begin with, and that with a little further instruction and practice he was able to win over his own creation. It will not do, however, to belittle the fact that there was a period when the machine was rather a consistent victor. It did win, and it did learn to win; and the method of its learning was no different in principle from that of the human being who learns to play checkers.

It is true that the choice of policies open to the checker-playing machine is almost certainly narrower than that open to the human checker player; but it is also true that the choice of policies effectively open to the human checker player is not unlimited. He may be restrained from a wider choice only by the bounds of his intelligence and imagination, but those are very real bounds indeed and not of a sort essentially different from the bounds of the machine.

Thus the checker-playing machine already plays a reasonably good game, which with a little further study of the end game and a little more skill in applying the *coup de grâce* may begin to approach master level. If it were not for the fact that the interest in checker championship has already been greatly diminished by the cut-and-dried nature of normal human play, the checker-playing machine might already be said to have destroyed the interest in checkers as a game. It is not surprising that people are already beginning to ask, will chess go the same way? And, when is this castastrophe to be expected?

Chess-playing machines, or machines to play at least an appreciable part of a chess game, are already in existence, but they are comparatively poor things. They do not, at their best, go beyond the level of a competent game between amateurs with no pretense to chess mastership, and they very seldom reach that level. This is largely due to the far greater complexity of chess than of checkers, both as to pieces and moves, and as to the greater discrimination between the policies suitable for the different stages of the game. The relatively small number of considerations necessary for mechanizing a checker game and the low degree of discrimination needed between its different stages are totally inadequate for chess.

Nevertheless, I find it to be the general opinion of those of my friends who are reasonably proficient chess players that the days of chess as an interesting human occupation are numbered. They expect that within from ten to twenty-five years, chess machines will have reached the master class, and then, if the efficient but somewhat machinelike methods of the Russian school have allowed chess to survive so long, it will cease to interest human players.

Be this as it may, there will be many other games that will continue to offer a challenge to the games engineer. Among these is Go, that Far Eastern game in which there are seven or more different levels of recognized mastery. Moreover, war and business are conflicts resembling games, and as such, they may be so formalized as to constitute games with definite rules. Indeed, I have no reason to suppose that such formalized versions of them are not already being established as models to determine the policies for pressing the Great Push Button and burning the earth clean for a new and less humanly undependable order of things.

In general, a game-playing machine may be used to secure the automatic performance of any function *if the performance of this function is subject to a clear-cut, objective criterion of merit.* In checkers and chess, this merit consists of the winning of the game according to the accepted rules of permissible play. These rules, which are totally different from the accepted maxims of *good* play, are simple and inexorable. Not even an intelligent child can be in doubt concerning them for longer than it takes to read them while facing a board. There may be great doubt as to how to win a game, but no doubt whatever as to whether it has been won or lost.

The chief criterion as to whether a line of human effort can be embodied in a game is whether there is some objectively recognizable criterion of the merit of the performance of this effort. Otherwise the game assumes the formlessness of the croquet game in *Alice in Wonderland,* where the balls were hedgehogs and kept unrolling themselves, the mallets were flamingoes, the arches cardboard soldiers who kept marching about the field, and the umpire the Queen of Hearts, who kept changing the rules and sending the players to the Headsman to be beheaded. Under these circumstances, to win has no meaning, and a successful policy cannot be learned, because there is no criterion of success.

However, given an objective criterion of success, the learning game may certainly be played, and is much closer to the way in which we learn to play games than the image of a game given in the von Neumann theory. Unquestionably the technique of the learning game is certain to be employed in many fields of human effort which have not yet been subjected to it. Nevertheless, as we shall see later, the determination of a sharp test for good performance raises many problems concerning learning games.

III

The learning to which we have been alluding so far is the learning of the individual, which occurs within the time course of his individual private life. There is another type of learning of equal importance—phylogenetic learning, or learning in the history of the race. It is this type of learning for which one type of basis has been laid down by Darwin in his theory of natural selection.

The basis of natural selection lies in three facts. The first of these is that there is such a phenomenon as heredity: that an individual plant or animal produces offspring after its own image. The second is that these offspring are not completely after its own image but may differ from it in ways also subject to heredity. This is the fact of variation and by no means implies the very doubtful inheritance of acquired characteristics. The third element of Darwinian evolution is that the over-rich pattern of spontaneous variation is trimmed by the difference in the viability of different variations, most of which tend to diminish the probability of continued racial existence, although some, perhaps a very few, tend to increase it.

The basis of racial survival and racial change—of evolution, as we call it—may be much more complicated than this, and probably is. For example, one very important type of variation is variation of higher order—the variation of variability. Again, the mechanism of heredity and variation generally involves the processes described functionally by Mendel and structurally by the phenomenon of mitosis: the processes of the duplication of genes and their separation, of their aggregation into chromosomes, of linkage, and the rest of it.

Nevertheless, behind all this fantastically complex concatenation of processes lies one very simple fact: that in the presence of a suitable nutritive medium of nucleic acids and amino acids, a molecule of a gene, consisting itself of a highly specific combination of amino acids and nucleic acids, can cause the medium to lay itself down into other molecules which either are molecules of the same gene or of other genes differing from it by relatively slight variations. It has been thought indeed that this process is strictly analogous to that by which a molecule of a virus, a sort of molecular parasite of a host, can draw together from the tissues of the host, which act as a nutrient medium, other molecules of the same virus. It is this act of molecular multiplication, whether of gene or of virus, which seems to represent a late stage of the analysis of the vast and complicated process of reproduction.

Man makes man in his own image. This seems to be the echo or the prototype of the act of creation, by which God is supposed to have made man in His image. Can something similar occur in the less complicated (and perhaps more understandable) case of the nonliving systems that we call machines?

What is the image of a machine? Can this image, as embodied in one machine, bring a machine of a general sort, not yet committed to a particular specific identity, to reproduce the original machine, either absolutely or under some change that may be construed as a variation? Can the new and varied machine itself act as an archetype, even as to its own departures from its own archetypal pattern?

It is the purpose of the present section to answer these questions, and to answer them by "yes." The value of what I shall say here, or rather of what I have said elsewhere in a more technical manner,* and what I shall sketch here, is that of what the mathematician calls an *existence proof.* I shall give one method in accordance with which machines can reproduce themselves. I do not say that this is the only method in which this reproduction can take place, for it is not; nor even that it is the manner in which biological reproduction takes place, for that it also is certainly not. However, different as the mechanical and the biological reproduction may be, they are parallel processes, achieving similar results; and an account of the one may well produce relevant suggestions in the study of the other.†

In order to discuss intelligently the problem of a machine constructing another after its own image, we must make the notion of image more precise. Here we must be aware that there are images and images. Pygmalion made the statue of Gala-

* *Cybernetics,* The M.I.T. Press and John Wiley & Sons, Inc., New York • London, 2nd ed., Chapter IX, 1961.

† The pattern of reproduction of genes by the splitting of a double spiral of DNA needs to be supplemented by an adequate dynamics to be complete.

tea in the image of his ideal beloved, but after the gods brought it to life, it became an image of his beloved in a much more real sense. It was no longer merely a *pictorial* image but an *operative* image.

A reproducing lathe can make an image of a gunstock model, which can be used for a gunstock, but this is merely because the purpose which a gunstock fulfills is very simple. On the other hand, an electric circuit may fulfill a relatively complicated function, and its image, as reproduced by a printing press using metallic inks, may itself function as the circuit it represents. These printed circuits have obtained a considerable vogue in the techniques of modern electrical engineering.

Thus, besides pictorial images, we may have operative images. These operative images, which perform the functions of their original, may or may not bear a pictorial likeness to it. Whether they do or not, they may replace the original in its action, and this is a much deeper similarity. It is from the standpoint of operative similarity that we shall study the possible reproduction of machines.

But what is a machine? From one standpoint, we may consider a machine as a prime mover, a source of energy. This is not the standpoint which we shall take in this book. For us, a machine is a device for converting incoming messages into outgoing messages. A message, from this point of view, is a sequence of quantities that represent signals in the message. Such quantities may be electrical currents or potentials, but are not confined to these, and may indeed be of a very different nature. Moreover, the component signals may be distributed continuously or discretely in time. A machine transforms a number of such input messages into a number of output messages, each output message at any moment depending on the input messages up to this moment. As the engineer would say in his jargon, a machine is a multiple-input, multiple-output transducer.

Most of the problems that we shall consider here are not very different or very much more different from those arising in single-input, single-output transducers. This might suggest to the engineers that we are dealing with a problem which he already knows very well: the classical problem of the electric circuit and its impedance or admittance or its voltage ratio.

This, however, is not exactly so. Impedance and admittance and voltage ratio are notions which can be used with any degree of precision in only the case of linear circuits: this is of circuits for which the addition of inputs as series in the time corresponds to the addition of the corresponding outputs. This will be the case for pure resistances, pure capacitances, and pure inductances, and for circuits composed exclusively of these elements, connected according to Kirchhoff's laws. For these, the appropriate input on which to test the circuit is a trigonometrically oscillating input potential that can be varied in frequency and can be determined in phase and amplitude. The output will then also be a sequence of oscillations of the same frequency, and by comparing it with the input in amplitude and phase, the circuit or transducer can be completely characterized.

If a circuit is nonlinear, if, for example, it contains rectifiers or voltage limiters or other similar devices, the trigonometric input is not an adequate test input. In this case, a trigonometric input will not in general produce a trigonometric output. Moreover, strictly speaking, there are no linear circuits, but only circuits with a better or worse approach to linearity.

The test input that we choose for the examination of nonlinear circuits—and it can be used for linear circuits, too—is of a statistical nature. Theoretically, unlike the trigonometric input, which must be varied over the entire range of frequencies, it is a single statistical *ensemble* of inputs that can be used for all transducers. It is known as the shot effect. Shot-effect generators are well-defined pieces of apparatus with a physical existence as instruments, and may be ordered from the catalogues of several houses of electrical-instrument makers.*

The output of a transducer excited by a given input message is a message that depends at the same time on the input message and on the transducer itself. Under the most usual circumstances, a transducer is a mode of transforming messages, and our attention is drawn to the output message as a transformation of the input message. However, there are circumstances, and these chiefly arise when the input message carries a minimum of

---

* Let me explain here what a shot-effect flow of electricity is. Electricity does not flow continuously but in a flow of charged particles, each with the same charge. In general, these do not flow at fixed intervals but with a random distribution in time, which superimposes on the steady flow fluctuations that are independent for nonoverlapping intervals of time. This produces a noise with a uniform distribution over frequency. This is often a disadvantage and limits the message-carrying power of the line. There are, however, cases such as the present, where these irregularities are just what we wish to produce, and there are commercial devices for producing them. These are known as *shot-effect* generators.

information, when we may conceive the information of the output message as arising chiefly from the transducer itself. No input message may be conceived as containing less information than the random flow of electrons constituting the shot effect. Thus the output of a transducer stimulated by a random shot effect may be conceived as a message embodying the action of the transducer.

As a matter of fact, it embodies the action of the transducer for any possible input message. This is owing to the fact that over a finite time, there is a finite (though small) possibility that the shot effect will simulate any possible message within any given finite degree of accuracy. Thus the statistics of the message arising from a given transducer under a given standardized statistical shot-effect input constitute an operative image of the transducer, and it is quite conceivable that they may be used for reconstituting an equivalent transducer, in another physical embodiment. That is, if we know how a transducer will respond to a shot-effect input, we know *ipso facto* how it will respond to any input.

The transducer—the machine, as instrument and as message—thus suggests the sort of duality which is so dear to the physicist, and is exemplified by duality between wave and particle. Again, it suggests that biological alternation of generations which is expressed by the *bon mot*—I do not remember whether it was Bernard Shaw's or Samuel Butler's—that a hen is merely an egg's way of making another egg. The liver fluke in the liver of the sheep is but another phase of a race of parasites that infects certain pond snails. Thus the machine may generate the message, and the message may generate another machine.

This is an idea with which I have toyed before —that it is conceptually possible for a human being to be sent over a telegraph line. Let me say at once that the difficulties far exceed my ingenuity to overcome them, and that I have no intention to add to the present embarrassment of the railroads by calling in the American Telegraph and Telephone Company as a new competitor. At present, and perhaps for the whole existence of the human race, the idea is impracticable, but it is not on that account inconceivable.

Quite apart from the difficulties of bringing this notion into practice in the case of man, it is a thoroughly realizable concept in the case of the man-made machines of a lower degree of complexity. For this is precisely what I am proposing as a method by which nonlinear transducers may reproduce themselves. The messages in which the function of a given transducer may be embodied will also embody all those many embodiments of a transducer with the same operative image. Among these there is at least one embodiment with a certain special sort of mechanical structure, and it is this embodiment that I am proposing to reconstruct from the message carrying the operational image of the machine.

In describing the particular embodiment that I shall choose for the operational pattern of the machine to be reproduced, I also describe the formal character of the pattern. For this description to be anything more than a vague fantasy, it must be expressed in mathematical terms, and mathematics is not a language to be understood by the general reader for whom this book is destined. Thus I must forego precision at this place. I have already expressed these ideas in mathematical language,* so that I have fulfilled my duty to the specialist. If I leave the matter at that, I shall have done less than my duty for the reader for whose eyes this book is intended. I shall appear to have asserted only some possibly empty claims. On the other hand, a full presentation of my ideas here would be utterly futile. Therefore, I shall confine my-

* *Cybernetics*, The M.I.T. Press and John Wiley & Sons, Inc., New York, 2nd ed., Chapter IX, 1961.

self in this book to as good a paraphrase as I can make of the mathematics that is the real heart of the matter.

Even at this I am afraid that the following pages will be rough going. For those who wish to avoid rough going at any cost, I must warn them to skip this part of the text. I am writing them only for those whose curiosity is sufficiently intense to induce them to read on despite such warnings.

IV

Reader, you have received the statutory warning, and anything you say in derogation of the following text may be used against you!

It is possible to multiply a machine, say a linear transducer, by a constant and to add two machines. Remember that we take the output of a machine to be an electric potential, which we may suppose to be read on open circuit, if we take advantage of the modern devices which are known as cathode followers. By the use of potentiometers, and/or transformers, we can multiply the output of a transducer by any constant, positive or negative. If we have two or more separate transducers, we may add their output potentials for the same input by arranging them in series, and thus obtain a compound device with an output any sum of the outputs of its component parts, each with an appropriate positive or negative coefficient.

We thus can introduce into the analysis and synthesis of machines the familiar notions of polynomial developments and of series. These notions are familiar in the case of trigonometric developments and of Fourier series. It remains to give an appropriate repertory of competent transducers for the formation of such a series, and we shall have given a standard form for the realization and, consequently, the duplication of an operative image.

Such a standard repertory of elementary machines for the approximate representation of all machines to what is, in an appropriate sense, any degree of accuracy is known to exist. To describe this in mathematical form is a matter of some degree of complexity; but for the benefit of the stray mathematician who may happen to peruse these pages, I shall say that for any input message these devices yield products of the Hermite polynomials in the Laguerre coefficients of the past of the input. This is really quite as specific and quite as complicated as it sounds.

Where can one obtain these devices? Not at present, I am afraid, as made-up devices in an electrician's supply house; however, they can be

put together according to precise specifications.
The components of these devices will be on the one
hand resistances, capacitances, and inductances,
familiar components of linear apparatus. Together with these, in order to obtain linearity, we
need multipliers which take two potentials as
inputs and yield a potential which is the product
of the two. Such devices are for sale on the market; and if they are somewhat costlier than would
be desirable in view of the number of them
needed, the development of invention may bring
the price down; and at any rate, expense is not
a consideration of the same order as possibility.
An extremely interesting device of this sort, working on piezoelectric principles, has been made in
the laboratory of Professor Dennis Gabor* of the
Imperial College of Science and Technology. He
uses it for a device which is different in many
ways from that which I have indicated but which
is also used for the analysis and synthesis of arbitrary machines.

To return to the particular devices I have mentioned, they have three properties that make them

* Gabor, D., "Electronic Inventions and Their Impact on
Civilization," *Inaugural Lecture*, March 3, 1959, Imperial College of Science and Technology, University of London, England.

suitable for the analysis and synthesis of the general machine. To begin with, they are a closed set of machines. That is, by combining them with appropriate coefficients, we may approximate to any machine whatever. Then they can be so proportioned as to be normal, in the sense that for a random impulse of unit-statistical strength they will give outputs of unit-statistical strength. Lastly, they are orthogonal. This means that if we take any two, give them the same standardized shot-effect input, and multiply their outputs, the product of these outputs, averaged over the shot-effect statistics of all the inputs, will be zero.

In a development of a machine in this form, analysis is as easy as synthesis. Suppose that we have a machine in the form of a "black box," that is, a machine performing a definite stable operation (one which does not go into spontaneous oscillation) but with an internal structure inaccessible to us and which we do not know. Let us also have a "white box," or a machine with known structure, representing one of the terms in the development of the black box. If then the two boxes have their input terminals attached to the same shot-effect generator, and their output terminals are attached to a multiplier that multiplies their outputs, the product of their outputs,

averaged over the entire shot-effect distribution
of their common input, will be the coefficients of
the white box in the development of the black
box as a sum of all the white boxes with appropriate coefficients.

To obtain this is seemingly impossible, as it
would appear to involve the study of the system
for the entire statistical range of shot-effect inputs.
However, there is an important accident that
enables us to circumvent this difficulty. There
is a theorem in mathematical physics which enables us in certain cases to replace averages over
distributions with time averages, not in every
single case, but in a set of cases with the probability 1. In the particular case of the shot effect, it
may be proved rigorously that the conditions for
the validity of this theorem are fulfilled. Thus
we may replace the average over the entire ensemble of possible shot effects, necessary to obtain
the coefficient of the white box in the development of the black box, by an average over time,
and we shall get the right coefficient with the
probability 1. This, though not theoretically a
certainty, is in practice equivalent to a certainty.

For this we need to be able to take a time
average of a potential. Luckily, apparatus for the
obtaining of such time averages is well known and

easy to procure. It consists only of resistances, capacitances, and devices for measuring potentials. Thus our type of system is equally useful for the analysis and the synthesis of machines. If we use it for the analysis of machines, and then use the same apparatus for the synthesis of a machine according to this analysis, we shall have reproduced the operative image of the machine.

This would seem at first sight to involve a human intervention. However, it is easy—much easier than the analysis and synthesis themselves—to cause the readings of the analysis to appear not as measurements on a scale but as the settings of a number of potentiometers. Thus, as far as the number of terms available and the precision of the engineering technique permit, we have made an unknown black box, by its own operation, transfer its pattern of action to a complex white box initially capable of assuming *any* pattern of action. This is in fact very similar to what occurs in the fundamental act of reproduction of living matter. Here, too, a substrate capable of assuming a large number of forms, molecular structures in this case, is caused to assume a particular form by the presence of a structure—a molecule—that already possesses this form.

When I have presented this discussion of self-multiplying systems to philosophers and biochemists, I have been met with the statement, "But the two processes are entirely different! Any analogy between life and the nonliving must be purely superficial. Certainly the detail of the process of biological multiplication is understood, and has nothing to do with the process which you invoke for the multiplication of machines.

"On the one hand, machines are made of iron and brass, the finer chemical structure of which has nothing to do with their functions as parts of a machine. Living matter, however, is living down to the finest parts which characterize it as the same sort of matter—the molecules. Then, too, the multiplication of living matter occurs by a well-described template process, in which the nucleic acids determine the laying down of the chain of the amino acids, and this chain is double, consisting of a pair of complementary spirals. When these separate, each gathers to itself the molecular residues needed to reconstitute the double spiral of the original chain."

It is clear that the process of reproduction of living matter is different in its details from the process of the reproduction of machines which I have sketched. As is indicated by the work of Gabor, which I have already mentioned, there are other ways of making a machine reproduce itself; and these, which are less rigid than the one I have given, are more likely to bear a resemblance to the multiplication phenomenon in life. Living matter certainly has a fine structure more relevant to its function and multiplication than that of the parts of a nonliving machine, though this may not be equally the case for those newer machines which operate according to the principles of solid-state physics.

However, even living systems are not (in all probability) living below the molecular level. Furthermore, with all the differences between living systems and the usual mechanical ones, it is presumptuous to deny that systems of the one sort may throw some light upon systems of the other. One respect in which this may well be the case is that of the mutual convertibility of spatial and functional structure, on the one hand, and of messages in time, on the other. The template account of reproduction is manifestly not the whole story. There must be some communication between the molecules of genes and the residues to be found in the nutrient fluid, and this communication must have a dynamics. It is quite in the spirit of modern physics to suppose that field phenomena of a radiative nature mediate the dynamics of such communication. It will not do to state categorically that the processes of reproduction in the machine and in the living being have nothing in common.

Pronouncements of this kind often seem to cautious and conservative minds to be less risky than rash statements of analogy. However, if it is dangerous to assert an analogy on insufficient evidence, it is equally dangerous to reject one without proof of its inconsequentialness. Intellectual honesty is not the same thing as the refusal to assume an intellectual risk, and the refusal even to consider the new and emotionally disturbing has no particular ethical merit.

For the idea that God's supposed creation of man and the animals, the begetting of living beings according to their kind, and the possible reproduction of machines are all part of the same order of phenomena *is* emotionally disturbing, just as Darwin's speculations on evolution and the descent of man were disturbing. If it is an offense against our self-pride to be compared to an ape, we have now got pretty well over it; and it is an even greater offense to be compared to a machine. To each suggestion in its own age there attaches something of the reprobation that attached in earlier ages to the sin of sorcery.

I have already mentioned the heredity of the machine and Darwin's evolution through natural selection. For the genetics that we have attached to the machine to be the basis of a kind of evolution through natural selection, we must account for it by variation and the inheritance of variations. However, the type of machine genetics which we suppose has room for both. Variation occurs in the inaccuracy of the realization of the copying process that we have discussed, while the copied machine exemplified in our white box is itself available as an archetype for further copying. Indeed, whereas in the original one-stage copying the copy resembles its original in operative image, but not in appearance, in the next stage of copying the spatial structure is preserved, and the replica is a replica in that as well.

It is clear that the process of copying may use the former copy as a new original. That is, variations in the heredity are preserved, though they are subject to a further variation.

V

I have said that the reprobation attaching in former ages to the sin of sorcery attaches now in many minds to the speculations of modern cybernetics. For make no mistake, if but two hundred years ago a scholar had pretended to make machines that should learn to play games or that should propagate themselves, he would surely have been made to assume the sanbenito, the gown worn by the victims of the Inquisition, and have been handed over to the secular arm, with the injunction that there be no shedding of blood; surely, that is, unless he could convince some great patron that he could transmute the base metals into gold, as Rabbi Löw of Prague, who claimed that his incantations blew breath of life into the Golem of clay, had persuaded the Emperor Rudolf. For even now, if an inventor could prove to a computing-machine company that his magic could be of service to them, he could cast black spells from now till doomsday, without the least personal risk.

What is sorcery, and why is it condemned as a sin? Why is the foolish mummery of the Black Mass so frowned upon?

The Black Mass must be understood from the point of view of the orthodox believer. For others it is a meaningless if obscene ceremony. Those who participate in it are far nearer to orthodoxy than most of us realize. The principal element in the Black Mass is the normal Christian dogma that the priest performs a real miracle, and that the Element of the Host becomes the very Blood and Body of Christ.

The orthodox Christian and the sorcerer agree that after the miracle of the consecration of the Host is performed, the Divine Elements are capable of performing further miracles. They agree moreover that the miracle of transubstantiation can be performed only by a duly ordained priest. Furthermore, they agree that such a priest can never lose the power to perform the miracle, though if he is unfrocked he performs it at the sure peril of damnation.

Under these postulates, what is more natural than that some soul, damned but ingenious, should have hit upon the idea of laying his hold on the magic Host and using its powers for his personal advantage. It is here, and not in any ungodly orgies, that the central sin of the Black Mass consists. The magic of the Host is intrinsically good: its perversion to other ends than the Greater Glory of God is a deadly sin.

This was the sin which the Bible attributes to Simon Magus, for bargaining with Saint Peter for the miraculous powers of the Christians. I can well imagine the puzzled aggrievement of the poor man when he discovered that these powers were not for sale, and that Peter refused to accept what was, in Simon's mind, an honorable, acceptable, and natural bargain. It is an attitude that most of us have encountered when we have declined to sell an invention at the really flattering terms offered us by a modern captain of industry.

Be that as it may, Christianity has always considered simony as a sin, that is, the buying and selling of the offices of the Church and the supernatural powers implied therein. Dante indeed places it among the worst of sins, and consigns to the bottom of his Hell some of the most notorious practitioners of simony of his own times. However, simony was a besetting sin of the highly ecclesiastical world in which Dante lived, and is of course extinct in the more rationalistic and rational world of the present day.

It is extinct! It is extinct. It is extinct? Perhaps the powers of the age of the machine are not truly supernatural, but at least they seem beyond the ordinary course of nature to the man in the street. Perhaps we no longer interpret our duty as obliging us to devote these great powers to the greater glory of God, but it still seems improper to us to devote them to vain or selfish purposes. There is a sin, which consists of using the magic of modern automatization to further personal profit or let loose the apocalyptic terrors of nuclear warfare. If this sin is to have a name, let that name be Simony or Sorcery.

For whether we believe or not in God and his greater glory, not all things are equally permitted to us. The late Mr. Adolf Hitler to the contrary, we have not yet arrived at that pinnacle of sublime moral indifference which puts us beyond Good and Evil. And just so long as we retain one trace of ethical discrimination, the use of great powers for base purposes will constitute the full moral equivalent of Sorcery and Simony.

As long as automata can be made, whether in

the metal or merely in principle, the study of their making and their theory is a legitimate phase of human curiosity, and human intelligence is stultified when man sets fixed bounds to his curiosity. Yet there are aspects of the motives to automatization that go beyond a legitimate curiosity and are sinful in themselves. These are to be exemplified in the particular type of engineer and organizer of engineering which I shall designate by the name of *gadget worshiper*.

I am most familiar with gadget worshipers in my own world, with its slogans of free enterprise and the profit-motive economy. They can and do exist in that through-the-looking-glass world where the slogans are the dictatorship of the proletariat and Marxism and communism. Power and the search for power are unfortunately realities that can assume many garbs. Of the devoted priests of power, there are many who regard with impatience the limitations of mankind, and in particular the limitation consisting in man's undependability and unpredictability. You may know a mastermind of this type by the subordinates whom he chooses. They are meek, self-effacing, and wholly at his disposal; and on account of this, are generally ineffective when they once cease to be limbs at the disposal of his brain. They are capable of great industry but of little independent initiative—the chamberlains of the harem of ideas to which their Sultan is wedded.

In addition to the motive which the gadget worshiper finds for his admiration of the machine in its freedom from the human limitations of speed and accuracy, there is one motive which it is harder to establish in any concrete case, but which must play a very considerable role nevertheless. It is the desire to avoid the personal responsibility for a dangerous or disastrous decision by placing the responsibility elsewhere: on chance, on human superiors and their policies which one cannot question, or on a mechanical device which one cannot fully understand but which has a presumed objectivity. It is this that leads shipwrecked castaways to draw lots to determine which of them shall first be eaten. It is this to which the late Mr. Eichmann entrusted his able defense. It is this that leads to the issue of some blank cartridges among the ball cartridges furnished to a firing squad. This will unquestionably be the manner in which the official who pushes the button in the next (and last) atomic war, whatever side he represents, will salve his conscience. And it is an old trick in magic—one, however, rich in tragic consequences—to sacrifice to a vow the first living creature that one sees after safe return from a perilous undertaking.

Once such a master becomes aware that some of the supposedly human functions of his slaves may be transferred to machines, he is delighted. At last he has found the new subordinate—efficient, subservient, dependable in his action, never talking back, swift, and not demanding a single thought of personal consideration.

Such subordinates are contemplated in Čapek's play *R.U.R.* The Slave of the Lamp makes no demands. He does not ask for a day off each week or a television set in his servant's quarters. In fact, he demands no quarters at all but appears out of nowhere when the lamp is rubbed. If your purposes involve you in a course sailing pretty close-hauled to the moral wind, your slave will never reprove you, even to the extent of a questioning glance. Now you are free, to dree your weird where destiny may lead you!

This type of mastermind is the mind of the sorcerer in the full sense of the word. To this sort of sorcerer, not only the doctrines of the Church give a warning but the accumulated common sense of humanity, as accumulated in legends, in myths, and in the writings of the conscious literary man. All of these insist that not only is sorcery a sin leading to Hell but it is a personal peril in this life. It is a two-edged sword, and sooner or later it will cut you deep.

In the *Thousand Nights and a Night,* the tale of the "Fisherman and the Jinni" is well to the point. A fisherman, casting his nets off the coast of Palestine, pulls up an earthen jar sealed with the Seal of Solomon. He breaks the seal, smoke boils out of the jar and takes the figure of an enormous Jinni. The Being tells him that he is one of those rebellious beings imprisoned by the great King Solomon; that at first he had intended to reward anyone who liberated him with power and riches; but that in the course of ages, he had come to the decision to slay the first mortal he might meet, and above all the man who should bring him freedom.

Fortunately for himself, the fisherman seems to have been an ingenious fellow, with a rich line of blarney. He plays on the vanity of the Jinni and persuades him to show how such a great Being could have been confined in such a small vessel by going back again into the jar. He claps the sealed lid on again, throws the vessel back into the sea, congratulates himself on his narrow escape, and lives happily ever after.

In other tales, the chief character does not have so accidental an encounter with magic and either comes even closer to the edge of catastrophe or incurs utter ruin. In Goethe's poem, *The Sorcerer's Apprentice,* the young factotum who cleans the master's magic garments, sweeps his floors, and fetches his water is left alone by the sorcerer, with the command to fill his water butt. Having a full portion of that laziness which is the true mother of invention—it led the boy who tended Newcomen's engine to fasten the valve string which he was to pull to the crosshead, and so led to the idea of the automatic valve gear— the lad remembers some fragments of an incantation which he has heard from his master and puts the broom to work fetching water. This task the broom carries out with promptness and efficiency. When the water begins to overflow the top of the water butt, the boy finds that he does not remember the incantation that the magician has used to stop the broom. The boy is well on the way to be drowned when the magician comes back, recites the words of power, and gives the apprentice a good wholesome scolding.

Even here the final catastrophe is averted through a *deus ex machina.* W. W. Jacobs, an English writer of the beginning of the present century, has carried the principle to its stark logical conclusion in a tale called "The Monkey's Paw,"* which is one of the classics of the literature of horror.

In this tale, an English working family is sitting down to dinner in its kitchen. The son leaves to work at a factory, and the old parents listen to the tales of their guest, a sergeant-major back from service in the Indian army. He tells them of Indian magic and shows them a dried monkey's paw, which, he tells them, is a talisman which has been endowed by an Indian holy man with the virtue of giving three wishes to each of three successive owners. This, he says, was to prove the folly of defying fate.

He says that he does not know what were the first two wishes of the first owner, but that the last one was for death. He himself was the second owner, but his experiences were too terrible to relate. He is about to cast the paw on the coal fire, when his host retrieves it, and despite all the sergeant-major can do, wishes for £200.

Shortly thereafter there is a knock at the door.

* Jacobs, W. W., "The Monkey's Paw," in *The Lady of the Barge,* Dodd, Mead, and Company; also in *Modern Short Stories*, Ashmun, Margaret, Ed., The Macmillan Co., New York, 1915.

A very solemn gentleman is there from the company which has employed his son. As gently as he can, he breaks the news that the son has been killed in an accident at the factory. Without recognizing any responsibility in the matter, the company offers its sympathy and £200 as a solatium.

The parents are distracted, and at the mother's suggestion, they wish the son back again. By now it is dark without, a dark windy night. Again there is a knocking at the door. Somehow the parents know that it is their son, but not in the flesh. The story ends with the third wish, that the ghost should go away.

The theme of all these tales is the danger of magic. This seems to lie in the fact that the operation of magic is singularly literal-minded, and that if it grants you anything at all it grants what you ask for, not what you should have asked for or what you intend. If you ask for £200, and do not express the condition that you do not wish it at the cost of the life of your son, £200 you will get, whether your son lives or dies.

The magic of automation, and in particular the magic of an automatization in which the devices learn, may be expected to be similarly literal-minded. If you are playing a game according to certain rules and set the playing-machine to play for victory, you will get victory if you get anything at all, and the machine will not pay the slightest attention to any consideration except victory according to the rules. If you are playing a war game with a certain conventional interpretation of victory, victory will be the goal at any cost, even that of the extermination of your own side, unless this condition of survival is explicitly contained in the definition of victory according to which you program the machine.

This is more than a purely innocent verbal paradox. I certainly know nothing to contradict the assumption that Russia and the United States, either or both of them, are toying with the idea of using machines, learning machines at that, to determine the moment of pushing the atomic-bomb button which is the *ultima ratio* of this present world of ours.

For many years all armies have played war games, and these games have always been behind the times. It has been said that in every war, the good generals fight the last war, the bad ones the war before the last. That is, the rules of the war game never catch up with the facts of the real situation.

This has always been true, though in periods

of much war, there has always been a body of seasoned warriors who have experienced war under conditions that have not varied very rapidly. These experienced men are the only "war experts," in the true sense of the word. At present, there are no experts in atomic warfare: no men, that is, who have any experience of a conflict in which both sides have had atomic weapons at their disposal and have used them. The destruction of our cities in an atomic war, the demoralization of our people, the hunger and disease, and the incidental destruction (which well may be far greater than the number of deaths from explosion and immediate fallout) are known only by conjecture.

Here those who conjecture the least amount of secondary damage, the greatest possibility of the survival, of the nations under the new type of catastrophe, can and do draw about themselves the proud garment of patriotism. If war is utterly self-destructive, if a military operation has lost all possible sense, why then the Army and Navy have lost much of their purpose, and the poor loyal generals and admirals will be thrown out of work. The missile companies will no longer have the ideal market where all the goods can be used only once and do not remain to compete with other goods yet to be made. The clergy will be cheated of the enthusiasm and exultation which go with a crusade. In short, when there is a war game to program such a campaign, there will be many to forget its consequences, to ask for the £200 and to forget to mention that the son should survive.

While it is always possible to ask for something other than we really want, this possibility is most serious when the process by which we are to obtain our wish is indirect, and the degree to which we have obtained our wish is not clear until the very end. Usually we realize our wishes, insofar as we do actually realize them, by a feedback process, in which we compare the degree of attainment of intermediate goals with our anticipation of them. In this process, the feedback goes through us, and we can turn back before it is too late. If the feedback is built into a machine that cannot be inspected until the final goal is attained, the possibilities for catastrophe are greatly increased. I should very much hate to ride on the first trial of an automobile regulated by photoelectric feedback devices, unless there were somewhere a handle by which I could take over control if I found myself driving smack into a tree.

The gadget-minded people often have the illusion that a highly automatized world will make smaller claims on human ingenuity than does the present one and will take over from us our need for difficult thinking, as a Roman slave who was also a Greek philosopher might have done for his master. This is palpably false. A goal-seeking mechanism will not necessarily seek *our* goals unless we design it for that purpose, and in that designing we must foresee all steps of the process for which it is designed, instead of exercising a tentative foresight which goes up to a certain point, and can be continued from that point on as new difficulties arise. The penalties for errors of foresight, great as they are now, will be enormously increased as automatization comes into its full use.

At present, there is a great vogue for the idea of avoiding some of the dangers, and in particular the dangers accompanying atomic war, by so-called "failsafe" devices. The notion behind this is that even if a device does not perform properly, it is possible to direct the mode of its failure in a harmless way. For example, if a pump is to break down, it is often much better that it do so by emptying itself of water than by exploding under pressure. When we are facing a particular understood danger, the failsafe technique is legitimate and useful. However, it is of very little value against a danger whose nature has not been already recognized. If, for example, the danger is a remote but terminal one to the human race, involving extermination, only a very careful study of society will exhibit it as a danger until it is upon us. Dangerous contingencies of this sort do not bear a label on their face. Thus the failsafe technique, while it may be necessary to avoid a human catastrophe, can most emphatically not be regarded as a sufficient precaution.

As engineering technique becomes more and more able to achieve human purposes, it must become more and more accustomed to formulate human purposes. In the past, a partial and inadequate view of human purpose has been relatively innocuous only because it has been accompanied by technical limitations that made it difficult for us to perform operations involving a careful evaluation of human purpose. This is only one of the many places where human impotence has hitherto shielded us from the full destructive impact of human folly.

In other words, while in the past humanity has faced many dangers, these have been much easier to handle, because in many cases peril offered itself from one side only. In an age where hunger is the great threat, there is safety in an increased production of food, and not much danger from it. With a higher death rate (and above all, a high infant death rate) and a medicine of very little effectiveness, the individual human life was of the greatest value, and it was appropriate to enjoin upon us to be fruitful and multiply. The pressure of the threat of hunger was like the pressure of gravity, to which our muscles, bones, and tendons are always attuned.

The change in the tensions of modern life, which results both from the rise of new strains and the disappearance of old ones, is rather analogous to the new problems of space travel. In the weightlessness that is imposed upon us in a space vehicle, this one-directional constant force, upon which we count so much in our daily life, is no longer present. The traveler in such a space vehicle must have handles to which to cling, squeeze bottles for his food and drink, various directional auxiliaries from which he can judge his position, and even at that, though it now appears that his physiology will not be too seriously affected, he may scarcely be as comfortable as he would like. Gravity is our friend at least as much as it is our enemy.

Similarly, in the absence of hunger, overproduction of food, purposelessness, and an attitude of waste and squandering become serious problems. Improved medicine is one factor contributing to overpopulation, which is by far the most serious danger confronting mankind at the moment. The old maxims by which humanity has lived so long—such as "a penny saved is a penny gained"—are no longer to be taken as valid without question.

I have been to dinner with a group of doctors—they were talking freely among themselves, and they were sufficiently self-confident not to be afraid of saying unconventional things—when they began to discuss the possibility of a radical attack upon the degenerative disease known as old age. They did not consider it as beyond all possibility of medical attack, but rather looked forward to the day—perhaps not too far in the future—when the time of inevitable death should be rolled back, perhaps into the indefinite future, and death would be accidental, as it seems to be with giant sequoias and perhaps some fish.

I am not saying that they were right in this conjecture (and I am quite sure that they would not claim it to be more than a conjecture), but the weight of the names supporting it—there was a

Nobel laureate present—was too great to allow me to reject the suggestion out of hand. Consoling as the suggestion may seem at first sight, it is in reality very terrifying, and above all for the doctors. For if one thing is clear, it is that humanity as such could not long survive the indefinite prolongation of all lives which come into being. Not only would the nonselfsupporting part of humanity come to outweigh the part on which its continued existence depends, but we should be under such a perpetual debt to the men of the past that we should be totally unprepared to face the new problems of the future.

It is unthinkable that all lives should be prolonged in an indiscriminate way. If, however, there exists the possibility of indefinite prolongation, the termination of a life or even the refusal or neglect to prolong it involves a moral decision of the doctors. What will then become of the traditional prestige of the medical profession as priests of the battle against death and as ministers of mercy? I will grant that there are cases even at present when doctors qualify this mission of theirs and decide not to prolong a useless and miserable life. They will often refuse to tie the umbilical cord of a monster; or when an old man suffering from an inoperable cancer falls victim to the "old man's friend," hypostatic pneumonia, they will grant him the easier death rather than exact from him the last measure of pain to which survival will condemn him. Most often this is done quietly and decently, and it is only when some incontinent fool blabs the secret that the courts and the papers are full of the talk of "euthanasia."

But what if such decisions, instead of being rare and unmentioned, will have to be made, not in a few special cases, but in the case of almost every death? What if every patient comes to regard every doctor, not only as his savior but his ultimate executioner? Can the doctor survive this power of good and evil that will be thrust upon him? Can mankind itself survive this new order of things?

It is relatively easy to promote good and to fight evil when evil and good are arranged against one another in two clear lines, and when those on the other side are our unquestioned enemies, those on our side our trusted allies. What, however, if we must ask, each time in every situation, where is the friend and where the enemy? What, moreover, when we have put the decision in the hands of an inexorable magic or an inexorable machine of which we must ask the right questions in advance, without fully understanding the operations of the process by which they will be answered? Can we then be confident in the action of the Monkey's Paw from which we have requested the grant of the £200?

No, the future offers very little hope for those who expect that our new mechanical slaves will offer us a world in which we may rest from thinking. Help us they may, but at the cost of supreme demands upon our honesty and our intelligence. The world of the future will be an ever more demanding struggle against the limitations of our intelligence, not a comfortable hammock in which we can lie down to be waited upon by our robot slaves.

VI

Thus one of the great future problems which we must face is that of the relation between man and the machine, of the functions which should properly be assigned to these two agencies. On the surface, the machine has certain clear advantages. It is faster in its action and more uniform, or at least it can be made to have these properties if it is well designed. A digital computing machine can accomplish in a day a body of work that would take the full efforts of a team of computers for a year, and it will accomplish this work with a minimum of blots and blunders.

On the other hand, the human being has certain nonnegligible advantages. Apart from the fact that any sensible man would consider the purposes of man as paramount in the relations between man and the machine, the machine is far less complicated than man and has far less scope in the variety of its actions. If we consider the neuron of the gray matter of the brain as of the order 1/1,000,000 of a cubic millimeter, and the smallest transistor obtainable at present as of the order of a cubic millimeter, we shall not have judged the situation too unfavorably from the point of view of the advantage of the neuron in the matter of smaller bulk. If the white matter of the brain is considered equivalent to the wiring of a computer circuit, and if we take each neuron as the functional equivalent of a transistor, the computer equivalent to a brain should occupy a sphere of something like thirty feet in diameter. Actually, it would be impossible to construct a computer with anything like the relative closeness of the texture of the brain, and any computer with powers comparable with the brain would have to occupy a fair-sized office building, if not a skyscraper. It is hard to believe that, as compared with existing computing machines, the brain does not have some advantages corresponding to its enormous operational size, which is incomparably greater than what we might expect of its physical size.

Chief among these advantages would seem to

be the ability of the brain to handle vague ideas, as yet imperfectly defined. In dealing with these, mechanical computers, or at least the mechanical computers of the present day, are very nearly incapable of programming themselves. Yet in poems, in novels, in paintings, the brain seems to find itself able to work very well with material that any computer would have to reject as formless.

Render unto man the things which are man's and unto the computer the things which are the computer's. This would seem the intelligent policy to adopt when we employ men and computers together in common undertakings. It is a policy as far removed from that of the gadget worshiper as it is from the man who sees only blasphemy and the degradation of man in the use of any mechanical adjuvants whatever to thoughts. What we now need is an independent study of systems involving both human and mechanical elements. This system should not be prejudiced either by a mechanical or antimechanical bias. I think that such a study is already under way and that it will promise a much better comprehension of automatization.

One place where we can and do use such mixed systems is in the design of prostheses, of devices that replace limbs or damaged sense organs. A wooden leg is a mechanical replacement for a lost leg of flesh and blood, and a man with a wooden leg represents a system composed both of mechanical and human parts.

Perhaps the classical peg leg is not interesting, as it replaces the lost limb only in the most elementary way, nor is the limb-shaped wooden leg much more interesting. However, there is some work being done on artificial limbs in Russia, in the United States, and elsewhere by a group to which I belong. This work is much more interesting in principle and really makes use of cybernetical ideas.

Let us suppose that a man has lost a hand at the wrist. He has lost a few muscles that serve chiefly to spread the fingers and to bring them together again, but the greater part of the muscles that normally move the hand and the fingers are still intact in the stump of the forearm. When they are contracted, they move no hand and fingers, but they do produce certain electrical effects known as action potentials. These can be picked up by appropriate electrodes and can be amplified and combined by transistor circuits. They can be made to control the motions of an artificial hand through electric motors, which derive their power through appropriate electric batteries or accumulators, but the signals controlling them are sent through transistor circuits. The central nervous part of the control apparatus is generally almost intact and should be used.

Such artificial hands have already been made in Russia, and they have even permitted some hand amputees to go back to effective work. This result is facilitated by the circumstance that the same nervous signal which was effective in producing a muscular contraction before the amputation will still be effective in controlling the motor moving the artificial hand. Thus the learning of the use of these hands is made much easier and more natural.

However, as such, an artificial hand cannot feel, and the hand is as much an organ of touch as of motion. But wait, why can an artificial hand not feel? It is easy to put pressure gauges into the artificial fingers, and these can communicate electric impulses to a suitable circuit. This can in its term activate devices acting on the living skin, say, the skin of the stump. For example, these devices may be vibrators. Thereby we can produce a vicarious sensation of touch, and we may learn to use this to replace the missing natural tactile sensation. Moreover, there are still sensory kinesthetic elements in the mutilated muscles, and these can be turned to good account.

Thus there is a new engineering of prostheses possible, and it will involve the construction of systems of a mixed nature, involving both human and mechanical parts. However, this type of engineering need not be confined to the replacement of parts that we have lost. There is a prosthesis of parts which we do not have and which we never have had. The dolphin propels itself through the water by its flukes, and avoids obstacles by listening for the reflections of sounds which it itself emits. What is the propeller of a ship but an artificial pair of flukes, or the depth-sounding apparatus but a vicarious sound-detecting and sound-emitting apparatus like that of the dolphin? The wings and jet engines of an airplane replace the wings of the eagle, and the radar its eyes, while the nervous system that combines them is eked out by the automatic pilot and other such navigation devices.

Thus human-mechanical systems have a large practical field in which they are useful, but in some situations they are indispensable. We have already seen that learning machines must act according to some norm of good performance. In the case of game-playing machines, where the permissible moves are arbitrarily established in advance, and the object of the game is to win by a series of permissible rules according to a strict convention that determines winning or losing, this norm creates no problem. However, there are many activities that we should like to improve by learning processes in which the success of the activity is itself to be judged by a criterion involving human beings, and in which the problem of the reduction of this criterion to formal rules is far from easy.

A field in which there is a great demand for automatization, and a great possible demand for learning automatization, is that of mechanical translation. In view of the present metastable state of international tension, the United States and Russia are filled with an equal and opposite necessity for each to find out what the other is thinking and saying. Since there is a limited number of competent human translators on both sides, each side is exploring the possibilities of mechanical translation. This has been achieved after a fashion, but neither the literary qualities nor the intelligibility of the products of these translations has been sufficient to excite any great enthusiasm on either part. None of the mechanical devices for translation has proved itself deserving of trust when momentous issues depend on the accuracy of the translation.

Perhaps the most promising way of mechanizing translation is through a learning machine. For such a machine to function, we must have a firm criterion of a good translation. This will involve one of two things: either a complete set of objectively applicable rules determining when a translation is good, or some agency that is capable of applying a criterion of good performance apart from such rules.

The normal criterion of good translation is intelligibility. The people who read the language into which the translation is made must obtain the same impression of the text as that obtained from the original by people understanding the language of the original. If this criterion may be a little difficult to apply, we can give one that is necessary if not sufficient. Let us suppose that we have *two* independent translating machines, say, one from English into Danish and the other from Danish into English. When a text in English has been translated into Danish by the first machine, let the second translate it back into English. Then the final translation must be recognizably equivalent to the original, by a person acquainted with English.

It is conceivable that a set of formal rules be

given for such a translation so definite that they can be entrusted to a machine, and so perfect that it will be sufficient for a translation to accord with these rules to be satisfactory as to the criterion which we have given. I do not believe that linguistic science is so far advanced as to make a set of rules of this sort practicable, nor that there is any prospect of its being so advanced in the predictable future. Short of this state of affairs, a translating machine will have a chance of error. If any important consideration of action or policy is to be determined by the use of a translation machine, a small error or even a small chance of error may have disproportionally large and serious consequences.

It seems to me that the best hope of a reasonably satisfactory mechanical translation is to replace a pure mechanism, at least at first, by a mechanicohuman system, involving as critic an expert human translator, to teach it by exercises as a schoolteacher instructs human pupils. Perhaps at some later stage the memory of the machine may have absorbed enough human instruction to dispense with later human participation, except perhaps for a refresher course now and then. In this way, the machine would develop linguistic maturity.

Such a scheme would not eliminate the need

for a translation office to have attached to it an expert linguist whose ability and judgment could be trusted. It would, or at least it might, enable him to handle a considerably larger body of translation than he could without mechanical assistance. This, in my mind, is the best that we can hope of mechanical translation.

Up to this point we have discussed the need of a critic sensitive to human values, such as, for example, in a translating system where all but the critic is mechanical. However, if the human element is to come in as the critic, it is quite reasonable to introduce the human element in other stages, too. In a translation machine it is by no means essential that the mechanical element of the machine give us a single complete translation. It can give us a large number of alternative translations for individual sentences that lie within the grammatical and lexicographical rules and leave to the critic the highly responsible task of censorship and selection of the mechanical translation that best fits the sense. There is no need whatever why the use of the machine in translation should leave the formation of a complete closed translation to the machine even in the sense that this translation is to be improved by a criticism as a whole. Criticism may begin at a much earlier stage.

What I have said about translating machines will apply with equal or even greater force to machines that are to perform medical diagnoses. Such machines are very much in vogue in plans for the medicine of the future. They may help pick out elements that the doctor will use in diagnosis, but there is no need whatever for them to complete the diagnosis without the doctor. Such a closed, permanent policy in a medical machine is sooner or later likely to produce much ill health and many deaths.

A related problem requiring the joint consideration of mechanical and human elements is the operational problem of invention, which has been discussed with me by Dr. Gordon Raisbeck of Arthur D. Little, Inc. Operationally, we must consider an invention not only with regard to what we can invent but also as to how the invention can be used and will be used in a human context. The second part of the problem is often more difficult than the first and has a less closed methodology. Thus we are confronted with a problem of development which is essentially a learning problem, not purely in the mechanical system but in the mechanical system conjoined with society. This is definitely a case requiring a consideration of the problem of the best joint use of machine and man.

A similar problem and also a very pressing one is that of the use and development of military devices in conjunction with the evolution of tactics and strategy. Here, too, the operational problem cannot be separated from the automatization problem.

Not only is the problem of adapting the machine to the present conditions by the proper use of the intelligence of the translator or the doctor or the inventor one that must be faced now, but it is one that must be faced again and again. The growing state of the arts and sciences means that we cannot be content to assume the all-wisdom of any single epoch. This is perhaps most clearly true in social controls and the organization of the learning systems of politics. In a period of relative stability, if not in the philosophy of life, then in the actual circumstances that we have produced in the world about us, we can safely ignore new dangers such as have arisen in the present generation in connection with the population explosion, the atomic bomb, the presence of a widely extended medicine, and so on. Nevertheless, in the course of time we must reconsider our old optimization, and a new and revised one will need to take these phenomena into account. Homeostasis, whether for the individual or the

race, is something of which the very basis must
sooner or later be reconsidered. This means, for
example, as I have said in an article for the
Voprosy Filosofii in Moscow,* that although science is an important contribution to the homeostasis of the community, it is a contribution the
basis of which must be assessed anew every generation or so. Here let me remark that both the
Eastern and Western homeostasis of the present
day is being made with the intention of fixing
permanently the concepts of a period now long
past. Marx lived in the middle of the first industrial revolution, and we are now well into the
second one. Adam Smith belongs to a still earlier
and more obsolete phase of the first industrial
revolution. Permanent homeostasis of society cannot be made on a rigid assumption of a complete
permanence of Marxianism, nor can it be made
on a similar assumption concerning a standardized
concept of free enterprise and the profit motive. It
is not the form of rigidity that is particularly
deadly so much as rigidity itself, whatever the
form.

It seemed to me important to say something in
that article which would emphasize the homeo-

* Wiener, N., "Science and Society," *Voprosy Filosofii*, No. 7
(1961).

static function of science and would at the same time protest against the rigidity of the social application of science both in Russia and elsewhere. When I sent this article to *Voprosy Filosofii*, I anticipated that there would be a strong reaction to my attitude toward rigidity; in fact, my article was accompanied by a considerably longer article pointing out the defects of my position from a strictly Marxist standpoint. I have no doubt that if my original paper had been first published over here, I would have had a similar and almost equal reaction from the standpoint of our own prejudices, which if not as rigidly and formally expressed are also very strong. The thesis which I wish to maintain is neither pro- nor anticommunist but antirigidity. Therefore, I am expressing my ideas here in a form that is not too closely connected with an evaluation of the difference between the dangers lying in these parallel but opposed rigidities. The moral I have wished to stress is that the difficulties of establishing a really homeostatic regulation of society are not to be overcome by replacing one set pattern which is not subject to continual reconsideration by an equal and opposed set pattern of the same sort.

But there are other learning machines besides the translation machine and the checker-playing machine. Some of these may be programmed in a completely mechanical way, and others, like the translation machine, need the intervention of a human expert as arbiter. It seems to me that the uses for the latter sort greatly exceed those for the former sort. Moreover, remember that in the game of atomic warfare, there are no experts.

VII

We have accomplished the task of showing many valid analogies between certain religious statements and the phenomena studied by cybernetics, and we have gone reasonably far in showing how cybernetic ideas may be relevant to the moral problems of the individual. There remains another field in which cybernetic ideas may be applied to problems with an ethical aspect: the cybernetics of society and the race.

From the very beginning of my interest in cybernetics, I have been well aware that the considerations of control and of communication which I have found applicable in engineering and in physiology were also applicable in sociology and in economics. However, I have deliberately refrained from emphasizing these fields as much as the others, and here are my reasons for this course. Cybernetics is nothing if it is not mathematical, if not *in esse* then *in posse*. I have found mathematical sociology and mathematical economics or econometrics suffering under a misapprehension of what is the proper use of mathematics in the social sciences and of what is to be expected from mathematical techniques, and I have deliberately refrained from giving advice that, as I was convinced, would be bound to lead to a flood of superficial and ill-considered work.

Mathematical physics has come to be one of the great triumphs of modern times. It is only during this century, however, that the task of the mathematical physicist has come to be properly understood, more especially in its relation to the task of the experimental physicist. Until the critical years from 1900 to 1905, it was generally considered that the main repertory of the ideas of mathematical physics had been completed with the work of Newton; that time and space, mass and momentum, force and energy were ideas grounded once for all; and that the future task of physics would consist in making models in terms of these notions for phenomena which had not yet been reduced to these terms.

With the work of Planck and of Einstein, it became clear that the task of the physicist was not so simple. The categories of physics were seen not to have been laid down once for all at the beginning of the eighteenth century, and the task of the physicist now has to be placed back of the Newtonian concepts, to bring our quantitative observations of the world into an order that should start with the experiments themselves and end with new predictions of observations and applied engineering techniques. The observer has ceased to be an innocent registrar of his objective observations but has, rather, come to take an active participation in the experiment. Both in relativity and in quantum theory, his role in modifying the observations is to be regarded as far from negligible. This has led to the birth of the logical positivism of the present day.

The success of mathematical physics led the social scientist to be jealous of its power without quite understanding the intellectual attitudes that had contributed to this power. The use of mathematical formulae had accompanied the development of the natural sciences and become the mode in the social sciences. Just as primitive peoples adopt the Western modes of denationalized clothing and of parliamentarism out of a vague feeling that these magic rites and vestments will at once put them abreast of modern culture and technique, so the economists have developed the habit of dressing up their rather imprecise ideas in the language of the infinitesimal calculus.

In doing this, they show scarcely more discrimination than some of the emerging African nations in the assertion of their rights. The mathematics that the social scientists employ and the mathematical physics that they use as their model are the mathematics and the mathematical physics of 1850. An econometrician will develop an elaborate and ingenious theory of demand and supply, inventories and unemployment, and the like, with a relative or total indifference to the methods by which these elusive quantities are observed or measured. Their quantitative theories are treated with the unquestioning respect with which the physicists of a less sophisticated age treated the concepts of the Newtonian physics. Very few econometricians are aware that if they are to imitate the procedure of modern physics and not its mere appearances, a mathematical economics must begin with a critical account of these quantitative notions and the means adopted for collecting and measuring them.

Difficult as it is to collect good physical data,

it is far more difficult to collect long runs of economic or social data so that the whole of the run shall have a uniform significance. The data of the production of steel, for instance, change their significance not only with every invention that changes the technique of the steelmaker but with every social and economic change affecting business and industry at large, and in particular, with every technique changing the demand for steel or the supply and nature of the competing materials. For example, even the first skyscraper made of aluminum instead of steel will turn out to affect the whole future demand for structural steel, as the first diesel ship did the unquestioned dominance of the steamship.

Thus the economic game is a game where the rules are subject to important revisions, say, every ten years, and bears an uncomfortable resemblance to the Queen's croquet game in *Alice in Wonderland,* which I have already mentioned. Under the circumstances, it is hopeless to give too precise a measurement to the quantities occurring in it. To assign what purports to be precise values to such essentially vague quantities is neither useful nor honest, and any pretense of applying precise formulae to these loosely defined quantities is a sham and a waste of time.

Here some recent work of Mandelbrot is much to the point. He has shown that the intimate way in which the commodity market is both theoretically and practically subject to random fluctuations arriving from the very contemplation of its own irregularities is something much wilder and much deeper than has been supposed, and that the usual continuous approximations to the dynamics of the market must be applied with much more caution than has usually been the case, or not at all.

Thus the social sciences are a bad proving ground for the ideas of cybernetics—far worse than the biological sciences, where the runs are made under conditions that are far more uniform on their own proper scale of time. For human beings as physiological structures, unlike society as a whole, have changed very little since the Stone Age, and the life of an individual contains many years over which the physiological conditions change slowly and predictably, all in all. This does not mean, however, that the ideas of cybernetics are not applicable to sociology and economics. It means rather that these ideas should be tested in engineering and in biology before they are applied to so formless a field.

Under these cautions, the familiar analogy of the

body politic to the body of the individual is a justifiable and a useful one. It is to the body politic that many considerations of ethics must apply, and to that part of religion which is essentially a paraphrase of ethics.

VIII

I have now run through a number of essays that are united by their covering the entire theme of creative activity, from God to the machine, under one set of concepts. The machine, as I have already said, is the modern counterpart of the Golem of the Rabbi of Prague. Since I have insisted upon discussing creative activity under one heading, and in not parceling it out into separate pieces belonging to God, to man, and to the machine, I do not consider that I have taken more than an author's normal liberty in calling this book

GOD AND GOLEM, Inc.

Index

[97]